JAMES J. MARSDEN

Joe Rogan: The Complete Biography

Biographies of Famous People [Volume 1]

First edition

This book was professionally typeset on Reedsy.
Find out more at reedsy.com

Contents

Introduction

Joe Rogan is a unique individual.

Joe is the modern-day renaissance man who achieved incredible success in more than one career. Joe Rogan is a stand-up comedian, fighting commentator and analyst, a successful businessman, and a podcast host.

Joe is a man of conviction, an idealist in his essence. Deep down, Joe is an explorer in constant pursuit of the truth. From the earliest age, his curious nature and wandering spirit led him on a journey of self-discovery.

Almost by accident, he became a martial artist when he was a teenager, and through the craft, he realized the importance of striving for excellence. Martial arts taught him valuable lessons about discipline, hard work, and sacrifice. All of these traits successfully translated into all of his subsequent careers, including stand-up comedy, acting, fighting commentating, and podcasting.

Due to his inevitable talent and magnetic charisma, Hollywood producers and executives took notice. Ever since he stepped foot into the spotlight, there was something unusual about Joe Rogan.

Throughout his life, Joe was never afraid to walk alone and carve his own path to success. From the moment he dropped out of college to pursue a career in stand-up comedy, he knew he was different.

His life choices certainly prove this notion.

Every time Joe found himself at the crossroads of life, he made choices that led to an unexpected turn of events. He was often ridiculed and doubted, but he always stayed true to his guiding values and principles in life.

Joe is one of the very few people who turned his back on Hollywood. More than 20 years ago, just when he was on the verge of breaking into the mainstream, he decided to follow his heart, and he never looked back. He took the road less traveled, and 20 years later, he arrived at the intersection of greatness.

Joe Rogan's triumph story is an example of the human spirit manifesting itself in a spectacular way.

Today, Joe Rogan is one of the biggest influencers in our society.

For many on the planet, Joe Rogan is the symbol and the last bastion of free speech. As such, he is targeted by global corporations, political groups, legacy media, and radical activists, effectively calling for his head.

Without a shadow of a doubt, Joe Rogan is one of the most polarizing figures of today. For some, he is a racist, a misogynist, a transphobe, a homophobe, and an anti-vax leader. Because of his willingness to have an open discussion and acknowledge different viewpoints, Joe Rogan is labeled as a great threat to public health and safety.

On the other hand, Joe has been an inspiration for millions of people. His reach and influence keep growing with each episode of the *Joe Rogan Experience.*

As the podcast host, he welcomed some of the most brilliant minds on the planet. He had conversations with people whose ideas have revolutionized society and people whose ideas transformed the way we live our lives. Scientists, doctors, philosophers, innovators, athletes, and many other remarkable human beings shared their stories with Joe and his faithful audience.

So...The million-dollar question almost imposes itself:

Who is Joe Rogan, really?

In this book, you will find a definitive answer.

Through Joe's life and career retrospect, we'll carefully analyze his unusual journey through the decades. We'll revisit the highs and lows of Joe's life, his struggles, and his glorious accomplishments.

Each chapter focuses on a specific time period in Joe's life. We will examine events and circumstances that shaped Joe into what he is today.

Without further ado, let's start from the beginning.

1

The 1970s and 1980s: Early Life, Martial Arts Prodigy & New Found Purpose

Joseph James Rogan was born in Newark, New Jersey, on August 11, 1967. His father, Joseph Rogan, was a former police officer who married Joe's mother when she was just a teenage girl. Right from the get-go, it was evident that the two of them were incompatible, and they had wildly different personalities.

Joseph Rogan Senior was a man hardened by the years he spent in the police force. In his essence, Joseph Rogan Senior was a strict conservative who demanded strict discipline from both his son and his wife. On the other hand, Joe's mother was a girl who wanted to live her life in accordance with her liberal values.

Joe Rogan's formative years were turbulent, as his earliest memories are of his father abusing his mother. As Joe recalls, his father was never physically abusive towards him, but young Joe was terrified of his father.

When he wasn't at home, Joseph Rogan Senior spent his time at his bar, drinking himself into oblivion. He insisted that his son Joe go to the catholic school and be introduced to religion from the earliest age. After all, the Rogan family had strong Italian-Irish roots, where catholic religion is a necessity for everyone, without exception. He grew up in an ethnic Italian environment, surrounded by many relatives.

As Joe remembers it, the surrounding was very much like 'Soprano's'.

At first, Joe was excited to go to catholic school as he believed God would protect him from the terror he experienced at home. Joe thought God would bring order into his chaotic life. However, Joe's experience with the catholic school turned out to be disastrous. He remembers crying and asking nuns for help and guidance. Instead of providing a 5-year-old with comfort, the nuns picked at him as they found his crying annoying and difficult to handle.

Luckily for Joe, his life turned around when his mother divorced his father. She would later meet the man of her dreams and remarry when Joe was seven.

Despite the tumultuous experience with his father, Joseph Rogan Senior shaped Joe's character and personality. Inadvertently, Joseph Rogan Senior taught his young son the lesson about parenting. More specifically, Joe Rogan swore he would use the negative example of raising children and do the complete opposite once he becomes a father.

In any case, it was finally time for Joe and his mother to be in a loving household. Joe's stepfather was on the complete opposite end of the spectrum than his biological father. As Joe describes him, he was a ''long-hair, weed-smoking, liberal hippie.''

He was also an architect student, and education was deeply ingrained into his essence. For that reason, the family moved to San Francisco, near the famous *Lombard Street.*

According to Joe, once they moved to San Francisco, his childhood was full of love and support. Both his mother and stepfather were a part of the hippie movement, a subculture movement that originated in the US in the early 1960s before spreading to the rest of the world.

Despite being at ease in his new home, young Joe Rogan remembers being constantly alone. Both his mother and stepfather were hard-working people, and even when they were at home, they would just watch tv as they were tired from work. Because of that, Joe had a lot of freedom from a very young age, and he would often wander the streets and explore the city of San Francisco.

From the earliest age, Joe showcased his curious nature and his wandering spirit. Little did he know at the time, but that curiosity directly shaped his life journey. Even though he was just a child, Joe was curious about history, sports, nature, and biology, and his family encouraged him by having regular conversations with him.

Both his mother and his stepfather treated him as an equal adult

3

during those conversations. They encouraged his curiosity and were there to answer all of his questions.

In many of his interviews, Joe explained his love for knowledge and his contempt for school. He was interested in certain subjects, while he perceived the rest of the classes as 'mental torture.'

One of the earliest passions Joe exhibited was towards art.

He loved to draw comics, and his early dream was to become a professional illustrator. Unfortunately for Joe, his art teacher somehow managed to kill the joy and the spark within him. The teacher would make fun of Joe's drawings and often belittle him in front of the entire class.

When Joe was 11, the family moved again. This time, it was *Gainsville, Florida.* The reason for moving was the same as the last time. Joe's stepdad wanted to further his education, and he enrolled at the *University of Florida.*

However, after only a couple of years, the family was on the move for the final time. They've settled in Newton Upper Falls, Massachusetts, outside Boston.

Despite moving quite often as a child, Boston is a place Joe considers home.

By the time Joe enrolled in Newton South High School, he had fallen in love with the game of baseball. He would participate in the Little League Baseball, and for a while, baseball would consume most of Joe's free time.

Around the same time, Joe developed an interest in martial arts. He dabbled in Karate for a while, but it was another contact sport that would become Joe's obsession.

Even though in those early teenage years, Joe seemed content on the outside, on the inside, Joe was a scared and insecure kid. Although it is somewhat usual for teenagers to feel insecure, Joe was terrified he would end up a loser.

When he was 14, Joe got into a physical altercation, and the outcome of that altercation changed Joe on a profound level.

During a lunch break, Joe got into a fight with another kid who threw him to the ground and decided not to punch him. It turned out that the other kid was a wrestler, and he knew how to fight. For Joe, the feeling of being helpless and left to the mercy of another was a feeling he never wanted to experience again in his life.

Although the event was traumatic and humiliating, it was also one of the life-changing experiences that Joe would forever be grateful for.

Just a few weeks after the incident, Joe and his friend went to the Boston Red Sox baseball game. After the game, instead of taking a bus, the two boys decided to walk home. Just as they were walking by a local gym, something made them stop and approach the window of the gym.

In a true moment of serendipity, and still, under the impression of humiliation he experienced recently, Joe heard a sound that would forever change his life.

He heard a loud thud, followed by the snap of the chain. It turned out that a man named *John Lee* was punching and kicking a bag. Joe Rogan stood there mesmerized and in disbelief of what was happening in front of his eyes. John Lee, a local taekwondo instructor, invited the two boys to join the training session.

Joe Rogan was fortunate to stumble upon one of the most prestigious Taekwondo schools in the US, *Jae H. Kim Taekwondo Institute.*

At age 15, Joe Rogan found a purpose in life. For the first time, he had clarity and a direction. For the first time in his young life, Joe didn't feel like a loser anymore.

In fact, Joe discovered he had a natural talent for the sport of taekwondo. In addition, it was through taekwondo that Joe discovered the value of discipline.

Within a few years, the name Joe Rogan became very well known within the taekwondo and contact sports circle. At the age of 19, Joe Rogan won the US Open Championship taekwondo tournament as a lightweight. He was a Massachusetts full-contact state champion for four consecutive years.

In fact, Joe Rogan became so proficient that he became a taekwondo instructor. He would regularly teach classes at Boston University, the closest he came to college graduation.

After graduating from Newton South High School in 1985, Joe became restless again. Despite not knowing exactly what he wanted to do in life, he knew exactly what he didn't want. He knew that a regular 9–5 job in the office wasn't for him.

By this time, Joe had already worked on construction, which was a job his stepfather managed to secure for him. He would spend a few summers working on construction sites across the US, and that heavy labor taught him the value of hard work.

In 1986, he took the entire year off before deciding on his next move. More specifically, whether or not he would pursue his college education. That year, Joe focused all his efforts on his martial arts career. In addition to taekwondo, Joe started boxing and kickboxing.

As soon as he did, he realized that he had a distorted perception of his fighting abilities. Other boxers and kickboxers would regularly beat Joe in sparing sessions. Disillusioned with taekwondo, Joe decided to quit and transition to kickboxing.

In late 1987, Joe was at a crossroads in his life.

The nagging voice at the back of his head emerged again, telling him he was a loser for not enrolling in college. Joe had no interest in pursuing his formal education, but he was afraid of the future, and college seemed like the most appropriate option at the time.

Joe's next stop was the University of Massachusetts in Boston.

As soon as the semester began, Joe realized he had made a massive mistake. However, he decided to push through the first semester. According to Joe, there was an event that ultimately

7

made him quit college for good.

After half of the semester, Joe received a phone call from the dean of the university. Apparently, they wanted to know why Joe was absent from school. They asked him to present a compelling case as to why they shouldn't expel him.

So he did.

Joe wrote a letter saying his life was difficult at the moment, but his desire to remain at the university was still strong. He remembers working so hard on that letter, and at one point, Joe faced the truth.

His heart simply wasn't in it.

He was lying to them because he was afraid of being a loser who dropped out of college. Joe recalls the thought that occurred at the moment. If he had put half of the effort into his studies, tests, and exams as he had in that letter, he would've easily graduated.

Then, it dawned on him.

Joe realized he didn't want to continue. With that realization came the serenity. Despite being afraid for his future, Joe knew he had made the right decision. He stayed true to himself.

Around this time, Joe started competing in kickboxing. As an amateur, he amassed a 2–1 record and was on the verge of turning pro. He certainly had a desire and a talent to become a professional, but some things in life are not meant to be.

Joe started to experience terrible and frequent headaches as a result of fighting and sparring in the gym. As much as he enjoyed fighting, the potential brain damage and long-term consequences were enough to deter Joe Rogan from pursuing his dream of becoming a professional fighter.

As soon as he closed that door, another one opened right in front of him. The universe seemed to nudge him in a completely different direction.

Throughout his martial arts career, Joe regularly used humor to alleviate the stress and tension. He would make his fellow fighters and teammates laugh and uplift the team spirit, especially before fights.

Joe recalls humor being a big part of his life. As he remembers, from the earliest age, he loved to get people to laugh and get a reaction from them. In elementary school, he would draw sketches and caricatures of his fellow students. He also drew teachers who certainly didn't appreciate it as much as the children. In any case, Joe would always get a reaction and a good laugh.

As he got older, he replaced the funny drawings with another medium, which was a verbal comedy. Years later, Joe Rogan admitted that he would have never dared to try stand-up comedy if his friends and teammates didn't encourage him to give it a shot. Joe remembers a man named *Steve Graham*, who was the most vocal and supportive. Steve was a little older than Joe, and he was the leader and the most respected man in the gym.

In other words, if Steve believed Joe had a solid chance in the stand-up comedy world, Joe had to accept it and believe it.

Joe was hesitant initially, as he never considered himself particularly funny. Before developing a certain comedy style, Joe was an excellent impressionist, and his impressions got the most laugh from his friends.

After six months of preparation, he performed his first stand-up routine on August 27, 1988, at an open-mic night at *'Stitches'* comedy club in Boston. To this day, Joe remembers this night clearly and vividly. Like all the other candidates that night, Joe had five minutes to deliver his routine.

He remembers how terrified he was before stepping up to the stage. Joe said he was so terrible and that he bombed hard. In the comedy lingo, the word 'bombed' means the comedian didn't get a reaction from the audience, and it usually refers to the entire comedy set.

Without a shadow of a doubt, the worst punishment for any performer, and especially a stand-up comic, is not getting a laugh from the audience.

Despite his lackluster debut, Joe fell in love with the craft.

He loved the adrenaline rush he felt when he was on stage, which is something he previously only felt when fighting. Unlike fighting, the biggest damage a performer could sustain in comedy was a bruised ego.

Around this time, he knew he had to make a choice between fighting professionally and stand-up comedy. The decision was quite easy for Joe, and he decided to hang up his gloves and retire from kickboxing.

After that fateful night in Boston, Joe Rogan finally had a long-term direction in life.

Although no one would've bet Joe Rogan would eventually become a comedy superstar, looking back, the writing was on the wall.

Joe's love for humor and comedy was certainly deeply ingrained in him.

Joe loved comedy from an early age; however, it was *Richard Pryor: Live on the Sunset Strip* that touched him on a profound level. According to Joe, nothing ever made him laugh like the movie, and especially Richard Pryor's comedy act. Joe's other comedy influences include *Richard Jeni, Lenny Bruce, Sam Kinison,* and *Bill Hicks*, among others.

Nowadays, comedians are much more supportive of each other, and the community is more inclusive, especially towards beginners. Back in the late 80s and early 90s, the situation was quite the opposite. The opportunities for stand-up comedians were scarce, and there was a general 'survival of the fittest' vibe around the entire community.

Today, thanks to the power of the internet, the price of admission is much lower, and the opportunities are in abundance for those willing to seize them.

11

In that pre-digital era and about a year after the beginning of his career, Joe was fortunate to meet a man name who would coach him and help him polish his stand-up material. That man was very well known in the Boston area, and his name was Lenny Clarke. Lenny is probably best known as *'Lenny,'* the titular character of the show that aired on CBS in 1990.

Just a week after Joe's debut in *'Stitches,'* another young man debuted in the same place. *Greg Fitzsimmons* became Joe's close friend, and the two of them would travel all around the country performing and honing their craft in the process. Needless to say that they weren't getting paid, but the effort both of them invested had to come to fruition eventually.

Years later, Greg would end up working as a writer for many prestigious shows and programs, including Louis C.K.'s sitcom *Lucky Louie*, *Politically Incorrect with Bill Maher*, *Cedric the Entertainer Presents*, *The Man Show*, *The Wanda Sykes Show*, *The Gong Show with Dave Attell* and *The Chelsea Handler Show*. Fitzsimmons was a writer and producer on *The Ellen DeGeneres Show*, for which he won four Daytime Emmys.

For a while, Joe had to take up odd and unusual jobs so that he could support himself while chasing a dream of making a living from professional comedy.

Although his martial arts days were behind him, Joe gladly taught private classes to those who could afford them. In addition to teaching martial arts, during those years, Joe worked as a newspaper deliverer, a limousine driver, construction worker, and he completed duties as an assistant for a private investigator.

Despite the financial struggle, Joe never complained or thought of quitting.

On the contrary, Joe was obsessed with the craft of stand-up comedy, the same way he was obsessed with martial arts. Because he succeeded at martial arts, Joe knew he could make it as long as he put in the time and the discipline needed to develop his routine.

Sure enough, in 1990, Joe Rogan had a lucky break.

One night, he was performing at the Boston comedy club, where he would regularly practice and refine his new material. That night, a talent agent named *Jeff Sussman* came from New York, looking for new and potential talents. Apparently, Jeff liked Joe so much that he offered him a representation right there on the spot.

That year, Joe moved to New York, where he would stay for the next four years. During that time, Joe almost exclusively worked on his comedy routine, delivery, and his writing. Joe developed a style of comedy popularly known as ''blue style comedy'' which is a style involving indecent and profane references. Due to his style, Joe managed to land multiple gigs at a bachelor's party and even strip clubs.

After four years in NYC, Joe Rogan became a proficient comedian and was ready for the next big step. Just around the corner, something much larger was waiting for Joe. His next stop...'The

City of Angels.'

2

The 1990s & 2000s: The Bright Lights of Hollywood

In 1994, Joe Rogan was a well-known name on the east coast comedy scene. However, back then, the entire stand-up community was far from the mainstream eye. To make it and earn a decent living as a comic, there was only one place to be. Los Angeles.

Joe's agent, Jeff Sussman, managed to secure his client a spot on the national television. During the late 80s and early 90s, MTV produced a comedy special named *'Half-Hour Comedy Hour,'* where many famous and less famous comedians were invited and given a chance to host the show.

For Joe Rogan, this was his make-or-break moment.

The fact that you are reading this book only means one thing — Joe Rogan did well. In fact, after his stand-up routine, he received an ovation from the audience in the studio. Furthermore, MTV studio executives immediately offered him a 3-year exclusive contract and a starting role in their upcoming game show.

Joe Rogan declined an offer, and his agent sent tapes to various networks inciting a bidding war in the process. Eventually, he signed a developmental deal with Disney. Just a few months after his MTV comedy set, Joe was cast in his first major acting role.

FOX studios developed a new tv show about baseball called *Hardball*. Joe played the role of Frank Valente, young and eccentric talent on a baseball team. The show had potential and was well received by a test audience, but unfortunately, it was canceled after just nine episodes. Looking back, Joe believes the reason for the cancelation was the involvement of an executive who decided to re-write the show. Also, the unnamed executive refused to collaborate with other writers, and he rejected any constructive feedback from the rest of the staff.

Around this time, Joe tasted the Hollywood lifestyle, and he hated it.

Years later, he described it as 'fake and pretentious.' He couldn't relate to other Hollywood actors, and soon, he would start avoiding them as much as possible.

Joe Rogan came from a different world, the world of stand-up comedy, where your authenticity is your only currency. In the stand-up world, you must be real and authentic if you want to succeed.

Naturally, Joe would continue his comedy career, and he would deeply immerse himself in the LA comedy scene. Joe quickly became a regular performer at *The Comedy Store* in Hollywood, which was the Mecca of comedy. The store owner, *Mitzi Shore*, was one of the most influential people in Hollywood at the time. As soon as she met Rogan, she would offer him a regular spot in the club, and the two developed a close personal and professional relationship.

After the cancelation of 'Hardball,' Joe didn't have to wait long for the next big opportunity.

Paul Simms, a well-known Hollywood writer and producer, pitched an idea to NBC's executives for a new project. During the 90s, sitcoms were at the top of their popularity. Every major network had at least one sitcom, as that was the way to guarantee viewership and attention.

In 1995, NBC launched a new tv show called *'News Radio.'* The executives and producers offered Joe Rogan the role of *Joe Garelli*, which he gladly accepted.

The premise of the show was quite simple. The focus was on the work lives of the staff of a New York City AM news radio station. It had an ensemble cast featuring *Dave Foley, Stephen Root, Andy Dick, Maura Tierney, Vicki Lewis, Khandi Alexander, Jon Lovitz, and Phil Hartman.*

The audience particularly well-received Joe Rogan's role as handyman and electrician Joe Garelli.

Interestingly, the role was initially offered to another comedian — *Ray Romano.* As fate would have it, Romano didn't gel with the rest of the cast despite his obvious talent. Ray's slow, dry and sarcastic style of comedy helped him land the role of his career, the role of *Ray Barone* in *'Everybody Loves Raymond.'*

Joe Rogan played the role of Garelli throughout the entire series run, from March 1995 – to May 1999, and appeared in all but one episode. Years later, Rogan admitted how much he enjoyed working on the show at the beginning, but Joe's enthusiasm slowly faded as time went on. In all fairness, that role enabled Joe much-needed financial security and the opportunity to work on his stand-up comedy while not on set.

In 1998, a tragic event made Joe question his life and career trajectory.

Joe's close friend and mentor in the acting business, *Phill Hartman*, was tragically killed by his wife, *Brynn Omdahl.* Phill Hartman was a comedy genius famous for his stint on *Saturday Night Live* show and many other roles in movies and tv shows.

Phill was one of the very few friends Joe had in Hollywood. From the moment they met on the set of 'News Radio', the two immediately hit it off. Joe described Phill as a big brother and a mentor who taught him a lot about acting and stand-up comedy.

Even prior to the incident, Joe was on the verge of quitting the show and committing solely to his stand-up career. The untimely death of his friend made Joe question his future and career choices. He decided to honor his contract on the show, and fortunately for him,' News Radio' ran for just one more season until its cancelation in 1999.

For most actors, the cancellation of their shows is a time for remorse. Lost income. Lost jobs. Lost identity. For Joe Rogan, it was an opportunity to go all-in with his true passion — stand-up comedy.

Just a few months later, Joe recorded his first stand-up comedy album in two shows at the Comedy Connection at Faneuil Hall in Boston. The special was named: 'I'm *Gonna Be Dead Some Day...*' and was officially released in August 2000.

During the early 90s, and just around the time he got his big break in Hollywood, Joe returned to his martial arts roots as the unexpected event changed his paradigm.

In 1994, Joe witnessed a fighting tournament event that would forever change his life. The sport of MMA (Mixed Martial Arts) was slowly introduced to the world, as a combination of striking, grappling, and ground fighting, incorporating techniques from various combat sports from around the world. Although the sport was known as *Vale Tudo* in Brazil, it was unknown to the rest of the globe.

The sport's popularity came when fighting promoters introduced the events in the US, and the sport evolved once officials established the basic rules.

In 1994, the **Ultimate Fighting Championship** (**UFC**), an American Mixed Martial Arts promotion, organized the event with a single goal of determining which fighting style was the best.

That night belonged to one man. The Brazilian named *Royce Gracie* won the tournament after beating four guys in one night.

What was particularly and even more fascinating about Royce was that he was significantly smaller than all of his opponents. He was also a master of martial arts that was unknown to the US, and the rest of the world, at the time — **Brazilian Jiu-Jitsu (BJJ)**

That night, Joe's entire belief system about fighting and mixed martial arts changed. He realized that a new martial art that could revolutionize the fighting landscape was on the horizon. Joe being the explorer that he is, decided to immerse himself in the sport of BJJ.

Once again, like so many times before and after, Joe was an early adopter. He started his BJJ journey in his late 20s under the legendary *Carlson Gracie*. Nowadays, BJJ is a legitimate sport and a self-defense discipline taught in martial arts schools worldwide.

However, in the 90s, many professional fighters didn't know about the BJJ, let alone fighting commentators and hosts. In 1997, Joe Rogan's obsession with martial arts led him to a completely new career path. His manager and agent, Jeff Susman, was a close friend of the UFC's co-creator and original producer, *Campbell McLaren*. The company opened a new position, and that position of backstage and the post-fight interviewer had Joe's name written all over it.

Even though Joe was already an established stand-up comedian and an aspiring actor, he decided to add another job title to his resume. Joe Rogan made his debut as an interviewer at *UFC 12: Judgement Day* in Dothan, Alabama, on February 7, 1997.

Joe's first term with the UFC lasted for around two years, after which he quit. Although Joe loved the fighting business and his gig, it was simply unsustainable for him to keep going. Fighting events were often held in rural places, and Joe had to cover all of the expenses himself.

Moreover, Joe's stand-up and his acting career were suffering.

As mentioned already, the end of the millennium marked a new beginning for Joe. Besides filming his first comedy special, In 1999, Rogan secured a three-album deal with *Warner Bros. Records* and began tentative plans to star in his own prime-time televised sitcom on Fox named *The Joe Rogan Show*.

The show, co-written by *Seinfeld* writer *Bill Masters*, was to feature Rogan in a role of a second-string sportscaster who lands a spot as the token male on a View-style women's show. Just as the show was about to enter production, Joe Rogan received an offer that would change his career trajectory and make him a household name.

NBC developed a new game show titled *'Fear Factor.'*

The executives believed there was only one man who could host the show. They approached Joe and his agent with the offer, and after initial skepticism from Joe, he decided to accept the offer.

The reason for Joe's hesitancy was the premise of the show.

Contestants were required to complete three jaw-dropping stunts in exchange for $50,000. Those who failed or backed out were eliminated from the competition. These stunts included consuming live spiders, sheep eyeballs, and maggots in pursuit of the prize.

The only reason why Joe accepted the offer to host the show was to observe anecdotes and stories and use them for his stand-up comedy. He was convinced that the show would not last simply because of its preposterous premise.

Little did Joe know at the time, but the show ended up being one of the most popular shows on the network, with an original run lasting for five long years. Moreover, the show was syndicated and started airing on other networks, including FOX, UPN, WB network, and cable channel FX.

Joe particularly liked the role of the host because he could coach the contestants through the entire competition. As a martial arts teacher, Joe was familiar with the underrated aspect of coaching his students through the mental struggle that fighting inevitably entails.

In a way, Joe Rogan was one of the very few people who was actually trained to be the host of the 'Fear Factor.'

2002 was an important year in Joe's life. Just as he was hitting a stride with his 'Fear Factor' hosting career and his regular stand-up shows, Joe received another offer he couldn't refuse.

In 2001, the UFC was acquired by the new management. The new president, *Dana White*, had big plans for the organization. Unlike the previous owner, who promoted the events as bloody fighting tournaments, Dana wanted to shape the UFC into a legitimate sport.

The road ahead of him and his team was long and uncertain, but Dana knew what the very first step on that road was.

Dana approached Joe, intending to rehire him and give him a new position in the company. This time around, instead of being a backstage interviewer, Joe would be a commentator, calling the fights in the octagon. Dana's move was quite simple:

- Leverage on his increasing popularity
- Appeal to Joe's love for the sport
- Use his deep knowledge of the martial arts

Luckily for them, Joe had a simple request the second time they came to offer him the commentary position. Joe didn't want any money. He wanted free tickets for fighting events, for himself and his friends.

Joe accepted a full-time paid job after about a few months and fifteen free gigs as a commentator.

Nearly 20 years later, he still holds the same position. In the meantime, Joe Rogan won multiple prestigious MMA awards, including *Wrestling Observer Newsletter Award for Best Television Announcer* twice, and was named *MMA Personality of the Year* four times by the *World MMA Awards*. More than his awards, his legacy is forever etched and intertwined with the sport of MMA.

Throughout the early to mid-2000s, Joe Rogan was a busy man.

In addition to his hosting duties for 'Fear Factor' and commentary duties for the UFC, Joe still performed regularly at the Comedy Club. In 2003, Joe became the new co-host of *The Man Show* on Comedy Central for its fifth season from August 2003, with fellow comedian *Doug Stanhope*, following the departure of original hosts *Jimmy Kimmel* and *Adam Carolla*.

Joe stayed on the show for only one season, as the viewership declined and Rogan and Stanhope had frequent disagreements with the producers. The show ended after only a year, and Joe was already out on a new adventure.

Around this time, Joe entered negotiations with various network executives to host his own radio show. Despite being open to the idea, Joe's schedule was fully booked, and he simply didn't have the time to commit to such an endeavor.

In May 2005, Rogan signed a deal with the *Endeavor Talent Agency*. Two months later, he filmed his second stand-up comedy special, *Joe Rogan: Live*, in Phoenix, Arizona. The special premiered on *Showtime* in 2007.

In 2005, *TMZ* broke the news that Joe Rogan would fight famous Hollywood actor *Wesley Snipes*. At first, the news seemed like a typical TMZ click-bate gossip until the reports from underground MMA forums confirmed the news.

In 2022, the concept of celebrity fights is far from uncommon, but back in those days, the idea of two celebrities squaring off in the octagon was unprecedented.

Wesley Snipes was one of the greatest action superstars of the 90s, with hit movies such as *Passenger 57, Rising Sun, and Demolition Man,* among many others. Snipes's most famous role is the one of *Eric Brooks*, better known as *Blade.*

Wesley Snipes is also a certified martial artist. He has been training in martial arts since the age of 12, earning a 5th dan black belt in Shotokan Karate and 2nd dan black belt in Hapkido.

Although he has been one of Hollywood's hottest commodities for a decade, Wesley's star was slowly fading with the beginning of the new millennium. His representatives reached out to Joe's agent Jeff Susman, and Joe was convinced the reason had to be Wesley's desire to revive his career. Joe agreed to a sanctioned MMA bout that would take place later in the year.

As Joe recalls, 'He trained like a madman' for the next five months, and he got into the best shape of his life, despite being in his late 30s.

Just weeks before the official announcement of the bout, Wesley Snipes pulled out from the contest. It turned out that the reason Snipes asked for a fight in the first place was simple.

He needed a quick payout to alleviate his debt. Around that time, it became publicly known that Wesley Snipes was under the IRS investigation for the alleged tax fraud. (Later found guilty and sentenced to three years in prison)

Snipes and his representatives came to the idea of challenging someone famous associated with the rising MMA sport. However, once they researched the opponent and weighed the pros and cons, they decided to back down from a challenge.

2006 marked a turning point in Joe's career. After five years and 144 episodes in total, 'Fear Factor' was canceled after a continuous drop in viewership. During these six seasons of television, Joe got more than enough stories for his comedy acts and solid financial stability from a hefty paycheck that allowed him to focus exclusively on his stand-up.

Joe hired his friend, *Bryan Redban*, to be his exclusive videographer. Brian was a stand-up comedian like Joe, and the two had a longstanding friendship that dated from the mid-90s. What was particularly fascinating to Joe was the fact that Brian was a self-taught videographer and media producer.

Brian had an entrepreneurial spirit, and in 2004 he founded his media company *Talking Monkey Productions*. For all these reasons, Joe hired Bryan and asked him to move to California, which was when the partnership officially started.

Around this time, Joe also decided to dip his toes into this new thing called *Youtube*. Rogan was always a believer in technology and an early adopter of the internet. He created his blog back in 2000, and he has been writing and publishing articles on his platform ever since.

In 2007, Joe Rogan was in the center of the scandal that ultimately re-shaped the landscape of the stand-up comedy scene.

In the late 90s and early 2000s, the Mexican man by the name *Carlos Mencia* was tearing through the comedy scene, quickly establishing himself as of the most brilliant comics of the era. Carlos managed to get secure a deal with *HBO* and *Comedy Central*, and he even managed to crossover into the mainstream media with acting roles in television shows *Moesha* and *The Shield*, and starring in the film *Outta Time* and the animated show *The Proud Family*.

By 2005, Comedy Central announced Mencia's own half-hour comedy show, *Mind of Mencia.* The show mixed Mencia's stand-up comedy with sketch comedy, much like *Dave Chappelle's Chappelle's Show*.

By the mid-2000s, Mencia became arguably, the most influential and powerful comic in the business. By 2007, this brilliant Mexican man named Carlos Mencia had the world at his feet.

Except, none of it was real.

Carlos Mencia had been plagiarizing his routine ever since he stepped on the scene. He has been stealing jokes and even the entire sets from *Paul Mooney, Dave Chappelle, Richard Pryor, and Jeff Foxworthy,* just to mention a few.

Even his name wasn't real. In fact, Carlos Mencia was born in Honduras as *Ned Holness.* He became 'Carlos' in 1988 when *Mitzi Shore,* the owner of The Comedy Store, suggested that Mencia change his first name from "Ned" to "Carlos" in order to appeal to Mexican audiences.

Ned couldn't care less about the accusations, as he dealt with them swiftly in the past. He would blatantly steal from less-known comics and threaten to end their career if they spoke up. After all, he had powerful network producers and executives on his side.

No one would dare to stand up to him, and speak up for himself and other comedians. No one, except Joe Rogan.

On February 10, 2007, Rogan confronted Mencia on stage at the Comedy Store on Sunset Boulevard and accused him of plagiarism. His friend and videographer Brian Redban recorded the incident and posted the video on Youtube.

Along with the video, Brian posted audio and video clips from other comedians, including *George Lopez, Bob Levy, Bobby Lee, and Ari Shaffir,* among others. Joe Rogan has also posted audio and video clips of Mencia's interviews and joke routines, comparing Mencia's routines to those of other comedians on his blog.

This incident wasn't the first, nor the last time Joe Rogan went against the grain and did things his way. Joe stayed true to himself despite the repercussions he knew he would inevitably face. Because he filmed the heated argument, the comedy store banned Joe for two years.

Moreover, his agency fired him as a client because the same

agency was managing Carlos Mencia.

For any other comedian, being blacklisted from the industry would be a fatal career blow, but not for Joe Rogan. In fact, this incident helped him get exposure, and his popularity started to rise from that moment. More importantly, Joe Rogan earned the respect of his fellow comedians for standing up to Carlos Mencia, a guy his peers notoriously disliked in the comedy scene.

This incident became known as the *"Carlos Mencia incident"* and would forever change the nature of stand-up comedy and the landscape of the scene. As a result, Carlos Mencia's career was effectively over that night as he was branded as a joke thief. After this incident, comedians were less likely to steal jokes or rip off fellow comedians, as they were well aware of the consequences.

Despite being banned from the Mecca of comedy, The Comedy Store, Joe Rogan kept working diligently, and he released his next special, *Shiny Happy Jihad,* in April 2007, through *Comedy Central Records.*

2008 was somewhat of a quiet year for Joe.

As usual, he was mostly working on his comedy routines in preparation for his next special. He was involved in a new project developed by CBS and produced by *Ashton Kutcher.* The show in question, titled *'Game Show in My Head',* was originally hosted by the comedian *Chris Kattan.* However, after the pilot episode, the producers contacted Joe and offered him to host the show.

Joe accepted the offer, intrigued by the show's premise. The show involved contestants who tried to convince people to perform or take part in increasingly bizarre situations for money. Contestants must perform a series of five "hilarious and embarrassing" tasks in front of strangers, which they are instructed to do by the host via an earpiece.

Ultimately, the show turned out to be a commercial and critical flop. After just eight episodes in early January 2009, the show was canceled.

Little did Joe know at the time, but 2009 turned out to be a year when his life changed, both personally and professionally.

3

The 2010s: Family Man, Trendsetter & The Most Influential Man On The Planet

Joe Rogan is a man who loves his privacy. Ever since he emerged in Hollywood in the mid-90s, he has tried to keep his personal life away from the spotlight.

In 2019, in an interview with Canadian physiologist *Jordan Peterson*, Joe shared personal information that was unknown up until that point. The two of them covered many different subjects, and Joe admitted his struggle to keep and maintain healthy relationships with women over the years.

Reflecting back on his youth, Joe realized he wasn't ideal boyfriend material. Since his early teenage years, Joe attracted the attention of the opposite sex, but ultimately any relationship was doomed to fail for a simple reason — Joe always put his career first.

When he was an up-and-coming martial artist and Taekwondo champion, he had a serious relationship with his first girlfriend.

As he remembers, things were going well for them until the moment she committed an act Joe deemed as 'sacrilege' — She insisted on having sex in the Dojo, where Joe was teaching classes.

For any martial artist, a training place is a sacred ground, much like a church for any religious person. Despite being a teenager driven by raging hormones, Joe declined, and soon after, he broke up with her. The breakup made him realize his priorities in life.

During his Hollywood years which included acting, hosting, and stand-up comedy, many rumors surrounded his relationship status as the general public wanted to know who Joe was dating. This issue became more prevalent with the rise of technology and the internet, as the forums were full of wild guesses and speculations.

Throughout his entire career, and up until the present day, Joe tried to keep his personal life and his family away from the spotlight.

We know the relationship Joe had with another TV personality and actress, *Jerri Manthey.* Jerry is probably best known as the contestant in multiple editions of *'Survivor.'*

In the late 90s, before both of them got their big break, they were a solid couple. However, by the end of that decade, they went their separate ways. During that time period, Joe got unwanted attention as people were speculating on the possible reason for the breakup.

Whatever the case may be, Joe learned his lesson and never spoke about his girlfriends and intimate relationships again...Until 2009.

In 2009, various tabloids and media outlets reported information that Joe Rogan was getting married to a woman named *Jessica Ditzel*. Soon after, Joe confirmed the news and said he was excited about the new chapter in his life. Even his die-hard fans and supporters were caught off guard by this information, as no one seemingly knew Joe was in a relationship.

Throughout the years, Joe was a strong opponent of marriage as an institution, which is why the news came as a surprise to many. In fact, Jessica gave birth to Joe's first baby daughter in 2008, after which Joe decided to marry her.

Who is Jessica Ditzel?
Jessica Ditzel was born on July 18, 1975, in Sugar Land, Texas. Ditzel is the daughter of **Jeff Conrad Ditzel**, a musician and a member of the popular Minneapolis band *Ditch Pickles*. She graduated high school in Colorado Springs in 1993 and later attended California State University-Long Beach.

Before marrying Joe, Jessica was engaged to the lead singer of R&B group *H-Town*, *Keven "Dino" Conner*. H-Town is known for its songs, *"Knockin' Da Boot," "A Thin Line Between Love & Hate," and "They Like it Slow."*

Jessica aspired to be an actress, and like many talents in Hollywood, she worked as a waitress while pursuing her dream. In fact, in 2001, while on the job, she met Joe, and the two instantly clicked. They had been dating for eight years before the engagement and eventual wedding in 2009.

Just a year after the wedding, Jessica gave birth to Joe's second child, another baby girl. Although Joe keeps the identity of his children a secret, it is well known that he legally adopted Jessica's daughter from her first marriage.

In 2009, Joe made a decision that will forever change his life and elevate his status to superstardom.

The decision was made out of necessity, as Joe Rogan moved back to California with his family, which was a decision he reluctantly made. According to Joe himself, he was frustrated and was looking for something to occupy his mind. That something was a weekly broadcast show in the form of a podcast.

Joe and his friend, and video producer Jamie Redban, discussed the possibility of entering into the podcast world for a while, and once Joe moved back to LA, the two finally made it happen.

On December 24, 2009, the first episode aired, and it had around 200 people who were watching it live. They had no idea that they were witnessing history in the making. Truthfully, no one could predict the magnitude and the eventual impact of this podcast at that moment. The first episode was marked with technical difficulties, including a mic problem and the issues with the USTREAM server, a platform that hosted the show.

In the beginning, the idea was for Joe and Brian to sit in front of the camera and microphone and talk about whatever came to their mind. No script, no preparation, just a conversation between the two. However, after a few episodes, they've realized that there are only so many subjects they could talk about before becoming repetitive.

The first guest to ever feature on the podcast was Joe's close friend and a fellow comedian, *Ari Shafir.* From this point, Joe's goal for the podcast was to bring people he liked talking to. Most of his friends at the time were actors, comedians, and individuals from the martial arts scene. The first guests on the podcast were people like *Eddie Bravo, Joey Diaz, and Duncan Trussell.*

As the podcast grew, Joe realized the show needed an official name. For the first eight months, the podcast didn't have a name. It was simply titled *Joe Rogan Podcast.*

In August 2010, the podcast got its official name: *Joe Rogan Experience,* which was an homage to the *Jimmy Hendrix Experience.* At the same point, the podcast began to grow in popularity. Joe realized the growth of the podcast was an opportunity to invite more notable guests to the show, resulting in the appearance of guests such as *Tim Ferris and Sam Haris,* proving that the show works with more than just comedians, actors, and fighters.

The turning point of the JRE was the addition of *Jamie Vernon* as the production assistant in 2013.

Until that point, Brian Redban was in charge of producing the show, but he couldn't keep up with Joe's insane work schedule. For that reason, Brian needed help with his workload, and Jamie Vernon applied for the position. Joe immediately liked Jamie's personality, and Joe first hired him as an intern.

After just a few episodes, it became crystal clear that Jamie Vernon was a bonafide expert in technology, including audio and video editing. More importantly, he could easily follow Joe's rigorous recording schedule and intensity, which is something very few people could do.

Pretty soon, it became evident that Brian Redban's role was obsolete, and he left the show to pursue other interests, mainly his stand-up comedy career.

Jamie's contribution to the exponential growth of the show is often underestimated. In addition to the technical skills needed for the job, Jamie came in with enthusiasm and ideas that would eventually revolutionize the *JRE* show.

As a matter of fact, it was Jamie's idea to create a Youtube channel and reach a wider audience. In January 2013, around episode 300th, Jamie created a Youtube channel titled *Powerful JRE.*

At this point, there weren't a lot of Youtube channels posting long-form content, especially not in a podcast format. Many internet marketers and experts that started to emerge with the rise of social media criticized Joe and his podcast, claiming that people don't want to listen to other people talking for two hours.

Joe couldn't care less what other people think of him, even if they were self-proclaimed experts. He loved his new project and invested the same intensity, dedication, and effort as he did with martial arts and stand-up comedy.

As soon as the Youtube channel was created, it began to explode.

The channel gained 100.000 subscribers in the first year and another 150.000 in the second year, totaling 250.000 by early 2015. As the channel grew, so did the notoriety of the guests. *Neil deGrasse Tyson, Vsauce, Kevin Hart, Jay Leno,* and others with a similar level of fame started to make regular appearances.

Joe Rogan was beginning to establish himself as the guy who could get famous individuals that the audience wanted to listen to.

JRE show was beginning to be seen as a revolutionary way for people to get information on someone they might admire. It was also a way to observe their favorite stars in their most natural state while having an authentic conversation with Joe. Previously, the only way for people to find out information on these celebrities were through thoroughly edited interviews or highly pressured paparazzi situation.

JRE show managed to promote the celebrities and showcase who they are without their fame, which was exactly what made the show unique and appealing to the wider masses. The show's initial success prompted *Syfy* channel (owned by NBC) to offer Joe a show on their platform.

'*Joe Rogan Questions Everything*' aired in July 2013.

The show covered topics discussed on his podcasts, including the existence of Bigfoot and UFOs, and featured several comedians, experts, and scientists with the aim of trying to approach the topics with an open-minded perspective. SyFy agreed to produce the show without a pilot episode. The production team gave Rogan some creative control over the program and aimed to present it in his own words where possible.

Despite the interesting premise and a solid viewership, the show was almost identical to *JRE*. After just eight episodes, *'Joe Rogan Questions Everything'* was canceled.

Before *JRE* took off in numbers and the overall impact, in 2011, Joe made his big-screen debut in his first major role as Gale in the movie *Zookeeper.* Joe was hesitant to accept at first, but his close friend, *Kevin James,* persuaded Joe to take the role in the movie. They worked together again in *'Here Comes The Boom'* in 2012. This time, Joe Rogan played himself in an action-comedy film centered around the MMA world.

In late 2015, the *JRE* show became the most downloaded podcast in the world, with over 16 million downloads per month. In addition to these staggering numbers, we have to mention the accumulated Youtube views. The number was well over 300 million at that time. It became clear that in the age of information, people turned away from the traditional mainstream media and turned their attention to the internet.

In the span of just a few short years, Joe Rogan became a worldwide household name, and his show *JRE* became the place for people to consume content and get the information they needed.

As his channel and podcast's reach continued to grow, people inspired by the JRE success tried to imitate Joe's podcast formula, hoping for overnight success.

Nowadays, the podcast is on the rise, and many people consume content via audio format.

Interestingly the rise of podcasts was a precursor for another market disruption that would occur a few years later. Sometimes around the latter half of the 2010s, we witnessed the emergence of audiobooks.

Truthfully, the need for audiobooks was always there, as they were first introduced in the 70s in the form of tape cassettes. In the early 2000s, tape cassettes were replaced with CDs. Now, in 2022, internet technology allows us to download a book in a matter of seconds. Today, you can easily find your favorite book, fiction and non-fiction alike, in an audio format, which was inconceivable back in 2010.

In many ways, Joe Rogan is the 'Father of Podcasting,' and with the emergence of the audio content consumption, he indirectly contributed to the rise of the audiobooks market.

While all of this might sound impressive, Joe was never the man who rested on his laurels.

In 2018, Joe released his second *Netflix* special, *Strange Times.* This was the second special Joe released for Netflix after the first one, titled *Triggered,* was released two years prior. Both parties seemed satisfied with the cooperation, and Joe was working on the third special he planned to release sometime in 2020, which unfortunately never came to fruition due to a global pandemic.

The year when the pandemic hit the globe provided many with an unexpected opportunity. The unexpected opportunity to re-evaluate priorities, dreams, aspirations, and the opportunity to re-evaluate life itself.

Despite purchasing a brand new home in Bell Canyon, California, in 2018, the Rogan family decided to relocate just as the pandemic gained momentum with strict lockdown policies being introduced worldwide. For Joe himself, the decision wasn't too hard to make, as he felt anxious and unease in Los Angeles way before Covid 19 emerged.

On one of his podcasts, Joe talked about the time he was the happiest and at peace. He recalls the few months he and his family spent in Boulder, Colorado, where he was the most productive while learning to appreciate peace, quiet, and nature.

Unfortunately for the Rogan family, once Jesica became pregnant, they decided to relocate back to LA. Despite not wanting to move back to Los Angeles, Joe realized the potential hazards of having a newborn child at such a high altitude, which the city of Boulder is known for.

Joe Rogan's love-hate' relationship with LA has been well documented over the years.

He came to the city in 1994 with nothing more than a dream and the will to see that dream come to life. Los Angeles is the place where Joe Rogan made a name for himself, and for the most part, 'The City of Angels' had been kind to him.

As he evolved as a person, so did the city he once loved dearly. According to many interviews Joe gave over the past decade, it's crystal clear that he is a man who prefers privacy, nature, and freedom of movement, which is something that Los Angeles couldn't provide anymore.

Once the Covid hit, Joe decided to move with his family to a more suitable place, and the choice was obvious. Like so many people who left California during the Covid era, Joe and his family settled in Texas. More specifically, Joe purchased a home on Lake Austin, in Austin, Texas.

Moving to Texas allowed Joe to reconnect with nature and pursue another one of his many passions, which is hunting.

Joe Rogan is an avid hunter, and for him, hunting was always a spiritual act. According to Joe, he mostly hunts Elks for nutrition reasons. Many animal rights organizations have criticized him, but Joe argued that he became a hunter after watching gruesome factory farming videos.

He didn't want to contribute to the suffering of animals, and he questioned the quality and the nutritional value of the meat coming from these mass-producing farms. Joe hunts his food, and according to him, one hunted Elk is enough for an eight-month food supply. For hunting purposes, he traveled all across the US, including Utah, Colorado, Montana, and New Mexico.

2021 was another successful year for Joe Rogan. It was the year Joe sold his first business.

Joe is well-known for his ultra-successful parallel careers in stand-up comedy, UFC commentating and fight analysis, and podcasting. What very few people know outside of his fanbase is the fact that Joe is a highly successful businessman.

In 2010, when Joe launched his *JRE* podcast, he failed to attract advertisers as back in those days, no one really saw the value of the podcast show. In 2011, Joe managed to land his first sponsor for the show.

In one of those seemingly pre-destined moments, Joe met *Aubrey Marcus,* who deeply admired Joe's work and achievements. Once they started talking, they quickly realized they shared many similarities and interests. Most notably, both are passionate about fitness, performance optimization and improvement, and the exploration of the human consciousness. The 15-minute meeting quickly turned into a few hours long conversation, where the two of them shared more than a few joints.

Joe is a strong advocate for legalized cannabis, and he believes it holds numerous benefits.

Joe hosted the documentary *The Union: The Business Behind Getting High* and was featured in *Marijuana: A Chronic History* and *The Culture High.* He also supports the use of LSD, psilocybin mushrooms, and DMT toward the exploration and enhancement of consciousness, as well as introspection. He was the presenter of the 2010 documentary *DMT: The Spirit Molecule.*

In addition, Rogan has an interest in sensory deprivation and using an isolation tank. He has stated that his personal experiences with meditation in isolation tanks have helped him explore the nature of consciousness and improve his performance in various physical and mental activities and overall well-being.

Not surprisingly, Joe and Marcus struck a friendship on that day. Furthermore, Marcus managed to secure the first-ever sponsor for the JRE show. Marcus's stepfather, *Steve Shubin*, is the founder and CEO of one of the most unusual business enterprises in the history of humanity.

In 1998, Steve founded *Interactive Life Forms LLC* — with their primary product, a sex toy *Fleshlight,* quickly becoming one of the top-selling pleasure products brands for men.

It's worth noting that the first-ever *JRE* sponsor was a company that produces sex toys, and within a few months, the company managed to double the investment they made in the show. The cooperation proved to be fruitful for both sides, as the initial investment helped Joe Rogan and *JRE* stay afloat in those early days of the show.

Joe and Marcus entered a business venture together, and in 2014, they co-founded a fitness and training company, *Onnit.* Firstly, they opened a gym in Austin, Texas, and after a while, they branched out and started producing a line of supplements and training equipment.

Onnit's most popular product is the *Alpha Brain,* a dietary supplement that helps support cognitive functions, including memory, mental speed, and focus. Joe Rogan is the product's most influential promoter, and you can often hear him talk about the numerous benefits he has experienced since he started using it.

Onnit continual success and exponential growth led to *Unilever,* a British multinational consumer goods company. As reported on April 26, 2021, on *Bizjournals.com*, Onnit agreed to a buyout with Unilever.

Unilever is the parent company of some very well-known brands, including *Ben and Jerry's and Axe.* Though terms remain undisclosed, many believe the deal was worth well over $100 million. Some estimate that number is closer to $250 — $400 million.

As the co-founder and the main investor, it is rumored that Joe earned between $50–$150 million from the sale.

4

The 2020s: The Public Enemy No. 1, The Witch Hunt & The War Against The Cancel Culture Movement

Because of the magnitude and the impact of Joe Rogan and *JRE*, and his willingness to have a conversation with anybody, he soon became a target for those who wanted to cancel Joe and his show.

Deep down, Joe Rogan is an idealist. He believes an open dialogue is the only way for our society to move forward, in spite of our differences.

In today's highly polarized society, that idea of free speech and open dialogue seems to go against the interest of certain individuals and powerful entities. These individuals include various activists and groups whose mission is to prevent information they deem 'dangerous' from reaching a wider audience.

Since 2017, Joe became a part of an influential yet highly

notorious group called *Intelectual Dark Web (IDW)*.

IDW is a loosely defined informal group of scientists, thinkers, authors, and commentators who oppose what they regard as the dominance of identity politics, political correctness, and cancel culture in higher education and the news media within Western countries. Those linked to the IDW have come from both the right and left of the political spectrum.

The legitimacy of the group was alleged in May 2018 in an opinion piece by then staff editor *Bari Weiss* in *The New York Times* titled:**"Meet the Renegades of the Intellectual Dark Web."**

She identified members of the network as highly influential personalities such as *Ayaan Hirsi Ali, Sam Harris, Heather Heying, Claire Lehmann, Douglas Murray, Maajid Nawaz, Jordan Peterson, Steven Pinker, Dave Rubin, Ben Shapiro, Michael Shermer, Christina Hoff Sommers, Bret Weinstein, and Eric Weinstein.*

Although Joe and some other alleged members denied the group had any actual influence and official agenda, the fact remains that many of the above mentioned are regular guests on *JRE*. Since 2017, there has been a significant backlash against IDW, mainly from the far left side, where the group is called a 'group of deplorable conservatives.'

Interestingly, Joe himself talked on more than one occasion about his political stance. Although CNN described Rogan as "libertarian-leaning," Joe Rogan has said that he holds a wide variety of political views and does not easily fall on any particular side of the political spectrum.

Joe has described himself as socially liberal, saying that he supports same-sex marriage, gay rights, women's rights, recreational drug use, universal health care, and universal basic income, but also supports gun rights and the Second Amendment.

Joe Rogan is a well-known advocate and supporter of free speech, and throughout all these years, his *JRE* podcast has had guests from all sides of the political spectrum.

Joe's desire to have a conversation with people he finds interesting is his only guiding principle. Everybody is welcome in Joe's iconic brick studio regardless of their political, sexual, or religious orientation. (As long as they have something worth talking about and an exciting story to share)

Joe Rogan was always a man of strong convictions, and unlike many celebrities and influencers, he never shied away from speaking about subjects he holds dear in his heart.

One of those subjects is the hot topic of transgendered people in sports and, more specifically, transgendered people in woman's sports. Joe publicly stated he believes an individual has every right to live the life they want to live, identify in a manner they believe is right for them, and that the rest of society should be respectful of their choice. However, for Joe, the line in the sand is the notion of trans women competing with cisgender women in all forms of amateur and professional sports, including MMA matches.

Over the years, he engaged several guests on his podcast in the civilized discussion, giving his take on the issue, but he also carefully listened to the counterarguments.

Joe Rogan Experience kept growing in numbers and reach, and mainstream media mostly portrayed Joe Rogan in a neutral manner. In a period of a few short months, that portrayal was about to turn into something much more sinister.

2020 was a hectic year for the entire humanity. Seemingly overnight, the world shut down, fighting the invisible enemy in the form of a virus coming from China.

Coincidentally, 2020 was also a turning point in Joe Rogan's life and career. In May that year, media reports emerged claiming that *Spotify*, an audio streaming and media services provider, signed an exclusive deal with Joe Rogan worth around 100 million dollars. The multi-year agreement gave Spotify exclusive rights to the *JRE* podcast, while Joe maintained his creative control over the process and production of the show.

In 2020, when the entire world was in lockdown, it seemed some places in the US were adamant about introducing draconian measures, all in the name of public health. In the midst of civil unrest and growing political division, Los Angeles and California as a whole saw the crime rate drastically increase.

Joe was one of the first public figures who questioned the measures' validity and efficacy, especially strict lockdown policies, which he believed could cause an epidemic of mental health issues not so long in the future.

During the pandemic, Joe seemingly became a public enemy number one. Not surprisingly, considering a significant amount of effort certain interest groups put into restricting and censoring a free flow of information under the guise of 'protecting the public interest.'

With the rise of technology and the internet, the way people consume information has changed. The traditional manner of watching TV and consuming the news had become a relic of the past. Controlling the flow of information and 'programming' the viewers became increasingly more challenging and difficult.

The status quo has changed.

Over the last few years, the traditional media networks saw a drastic decrease in viewership. In late 2021, Nielsen Media Research published viewership reports and media ratings for the third quarter of that year.

Fox News topped the third-quarter ratings as well as September numbers, but all of the cable news networks showed year-over-year declines.

In the third quarter primetime, Fox News averaged 2.37 million total viewers, down 32% from the same period a year earlier. MSNBC posted 1.27 million, down 40%, while CNN had 822,000, down 46%. In the 25–54 demo, Fox News averaged 377,000, down 37%; CNN posted 188,000, down 52%; and MSNBC was at 161,000, down 51%.

The numbers are from Nielsen and were released by Fox News

and CNN.

In total day, Fox News averaged 1.36 million viewers, down 22%; MSNBC averaged 738,000, down 39%; and CNN had 598,000, down 38%. In the 25–54 demo, Fox News posted 227,000, down 25%, compared to CNN with 130,000, off by 46%, and MSNBC with 94,000, a drop of 48%.

Tucker Carlson Tonight once again topped total viewers with 3.24 million, followed by *The Five* with 2.98 million, *Hannity* with 2.94 million, *The Ingraham Angle* with 2.35 million, and *The Rachel Maddow Show* at 2.20 million. In the 25–54 demo, *Tucker Carlson Tonight* topped with an average of 549,000, followed by *Hannity* with 478,000, *The Five* with 478,000, *The Ingraham Angle* with 400,000, and *Special Report with Bret Baier* at 335,000.

However, these numbers pale in comparison with Rogan's JRE reach.

Truthfully, estimating the exact number may be an impossible task, considering that Spotify doesn't release viewership numbers, and Nielsen Metric includes only cable networks. However, in an interview with Jordan Peterson, Joe Rogan confirmed he reaches about 11 million people per episode.

Joe casually disclosed these numbers, seemingly unaware of their significance. In addition to podcast numbers, to get the complete picture of Joe's influence, we must consider his omnipresence on the internet. His Youtube channel has more than 12 million subscribers and more than 2 Billion views in total, Joe's Twitter account totals 9 million followers, his Instagram

15 million, and his Facebook 7 million followers.

With these numbers behind him, Joe Rogan is certainly a formidable opponent of the establishment. His willingness to seek the truth by having an open dialogue is what makes him dangerous.

In 2020, Joe attracted the wrath of a movement that relatively recently became a phenomenon in our society — Social Justice Warriors.

The term 'Social Justice' has been with us for a while, as the first time it's been used traces back to 1824. **Social justice** is justice in terms of the distribution of wealth, opportunities, and privileges within a society. From the early 1990s to the early 2000s, a *social-justice warrior* was used as a neutral or complimentary phrase. However, with the rise of the internet and digital globalization, the term switched from a positive to an overwhelmingly negative one.

Today, a Social justice warrior (SJW) is a pejorative term used for an individual who promotes socially progressive, left-wing and liberal views, including feminism, civil rights, gay and transgender rights, identity politics, political correctness, and multiculturalism.

The accusation that somebody is an SJW implies that they are pursuing personal validation rather than any deep-seated conviction and engaging in disingenuous arguments. The social justice warriors movement is deeply intertwined with another relatively recent phenomenon: *The Cancel Culture.*

The essence of the cancel culture is to call out an individual whose past behavior was reprehensible and hold them account-able for their actions. One of the first instances of cancel culture in action was with the rise of the #metoo movement, where victims finally got a chance to be heard. In 2017, more than 80 women spoke up against one of the most powerful and influential people in Hollywood, *Harvey Weinstein*, accusing him of sexual harassment and rape.

Quickly after the allegations were made, Weinstein lost his position in Hollywood. He was sentenced to 23 years in prison for his crimes, finally bringing justice to his victims. Many powerful people from all walks of life were called out, and many of them were, in fact, canceled.

However, somewhere along the lines, the noble idea of account-ability was twisted and used as a tool against anyone who holds different views. It became a vogue for public shaming and ostracism, with the tendency to dissolve complex policy issues in a blinding moral certainty.

One of the most effective methods of the so-called social justice warriors and the cancel culture online mob is to dig deep into an individual's past, meticulously looking for anything they can use to further their argument and ostracize the individual in question. The method usually involves scouring the individual's online footprint, including their public posts, images, videos, or comments.

In that process, they willingly disregard the most essential element before making an accusation—the context.

Once they find something they deem inappropriate or offen-sive, immediately the coordinated online campaign, usually on Twitter, starts spreading like wildfire, calling for that individual to be 'canceled' from society. This 'cancelation' is a form of ostracism in which an accused individual faces serious and tangible consequences.

In some cases, they are fired from their workplace due to external pressure and actively prevented from getting another job, effectively robbing them of their livelihood. In many cases, they become victims of online bullying and harassment, with their public information becoming available for everyone to see on the internet.

Victims of social justice warriors and the cancel culture often seek professional help and therapy, and it can take years for them to work on their issues and get better.

In any case, the victims of the cancel culture are left with a significantly smaller following and an overall influence. They are also left with a forever tarnished reputation, which is the main currency of any public figure.

During the Covid pandemic, an already polarized society saw a further division when a new term, 'Anti-Vax,' was introduced to describe those skeptical about vaccine efficacy and worried about the short-term and long-term consequences.

Somehow, those who are deemed as 'Anti-Vax' were immedi-ately put in the same group as those who believe the earth is flat, the moon landing was fake, and many, many other officially accepted narratives.

All these individuals and groups are often collectively called conspiracy theorists. If the mainstream media is to be trusted, these conspiracy theorists are nothing more than a fringe minority seeking to disrupt the collective progress of society.

During the pandemic, 'Anti-Vaxxers' became the most dangerous conspiracy theorists, and they were labeled as the biggest threat to public health and safety. The mainstream media identified the most influential individual and de facto 'leader' of this movement, which turned out to be, Joe Rogan.

In April 2021, Joe Rogan came under scrutiny when he expressed his belief that young, healthy people shouldn't get a vaccine, as their natural immune system is the best defense against a virus, a stance shared by many health care professionals and epidemiologists.

Five months later, On September 1, 2021, Rogan tested positive for the virus. Soon after, he released an online video reporting on the status of his condition and stating that he had begun a regimen including monoclonal antibodies, prednisone, azithromycin, NAD drip, a vitamin drip, as well as ivermectin.

CNN picked up a story and uploaded the same video of Joe to their site. However, the version of the video they uploaded was different. Looking at two videos side by side, it's evident that the one uploaded by CNN made Joe look grayish and lack proper facial skin coloration. The only problem for the video editors was the background behind Joe.

In an original video, the leaves on the tree have a natural green color, while in the edited version, those same leaves had an almost faded yellow/grayish color. What is even more despicable was the headline beneath saying: **'Joe Rogan treating Covid with horse dewormer.'**

Joe immediately called them on their lie, while *Associated Press* 'fact-checked' Joe's claim, announcing it to be false, despite the two videos side by side showing a clear difference in color and overall saturation. Within a few days, Joe Rogan fully recovered from Covid and tested negative for the virus. However, this wouldn't be the last accusation against Joe for spreading 'Covid misinformation.'

On December 21, 2021, in episode #1757, Joe Rogan welcomed a new guest on his *JRE* show. For the first time in *JRE* history, the guest was *Dr. Robert Malone.*

Dr. Robert Malone is the inventor of the nine original mRNA vaccine patents, which were originally filed in 1989 (including both the idea of mRNA vaccines and the original proof of principle experiments) and RNA transfection. Dr. Malone has close to 100 peer-reviewed publications, which have been cited over 12,000 times. Since January 2020, Dr. Malone has been leading a large team focused on clinical research design, drug development, computer modeling and mechanisms of action of repurposed drugs for the treatment of Covid-19.

Dr. Malone is the Medical Director of The Unity Project, a group of 300 organizations across the US standing against mandated Covid vaccines for children. He is also the President of the

Global Covid Summit, an organization of over 16,000 doctors and scientists committed to speaking truth to power about Covid pandemic research and treatment.

Joe and Dr. Malone spoke for more than three hours on a variety of topics related to Covid 19. The conversation certainly raised a lot of ethical questions that were somehow left unanswered by legacy media, health experts, and officials. Those same entities that continuously promoted the narrative that vaccines are the only way to return to 'the old way of living'; While at the same time publicly shamed, mocked, and ostracized those who raised a single question in regards to the official narrative.

Needless to say, the backlash from this episode was enormous. This time, *Rolling Stone* magazine labeled Joe Rogan as the **'Menace to Public Health.'**

At the same, allegedly, Spotify received an open letter from more than 200 scientists, physicians, professors, doctors, and healthcare workers expressing concern over "false and societally harmful assertions" on *The Joe Rogan Experience* and asked Spotify to establish a clear and public policy to moderate misinformation on its platform.

The signatories took issue with Rogan "broadcasting misinformation, particularly regarding the Covid 19 pandemic" and, more specifically, a highly controversial episode featuring guest Robert W. Malone.

The episode has been criticized for promoting "baseless conspiracy theories, including an unfounded theory that societal leaders have hypnotized the public.''

The signatories further assert that "Dr. Malone is one of two recent JRE guests who has compared pandemic policies to the Holocaust. These actions are not only objectionable and offensive, but also medically and culturally dangerous." The signatories also note that Malone was suspended from Twitter "for spreading misinformation about Covid 19."

Just a few weeks later, the Rock & Roll legend, *Neil Young*, posted an open letter threatening Spotify to censor *JRE* for spreading misinformation and lies about Covid 19. He went as far as giving an ultimatum to Spotify to remove his music catalog if they decide against censoring Joe Rogan. Soon after, Neil's good friend, Jenni Mitchel, joined in solidarity, and the two of them removed their music from the streaming platform.

To mitigate the damage and appease the outraged, Spotify swiftly reacted. In addition to removing many of the JRE episodes, Spotify added a disclaimer to each episode that con-tained information about the Covid pandemic.

Joe Rogan issued an apology in an Instagram video, reiterating his belief and vision for the JRE podcast, which is to provide a platform for an open and honest discussion. Joe declared his only goal was to get to the truth, and he invited those who hold different views to come to his show.

Joe's apology video served as an admission of guilt for the cancel culture mob, who in the upcoming weeks doubled down with the various online petitions and Twitter hashtags in a desperate

JOE ROGAN: THE COMPLETE BIOGRAPHY

attempt to remove Joe Rogan from the internet.

As the Coronavirus fearmongering began to wane and many countries around the world started easing and removing the Covid measures, Joe Rogan found himself in the crosshairs yet again. In addition to being labeled a 'homophobe,' 'transphobe,' 'misogynist,' and a 'deplorable conservative,' Joe earned himself a brand new label —'a racist.'

In February 2022, a video compilation of Joe Rogan taken from various *JRE* episodes and stitched together in a single video, in which he says the infamous 'N-word' multiple times, emerged and went viral. The legacy media, including CNN and MSNBC, led the attack, with the usual cancel mob following the charge on social media.

Although many celebrities, including UFC champion *Israel Adesanya,* a former UFC champion *Rashad Evans,* martial artist and actor *Michael Jai White,* offered unconditional support to Joe Rogan, the man himself issued another apology.

In another Instagram video, Joe apologized for his words calling his past language shameful and regretful. Joe also added that the video compilation contains clips taken out of the context and that he only quoted the word to discuss it with others.

Since then, the storm has quieted down...Until a new one inevitably arrives on the horizon.

5

Joe Rogan: Unfiltered and Raw

Joe Rogan has captured the attention and imagination of people across the globe ever since stepping out into the spotlight.

He influenced millions over the last decade since the first episode of *JRE* hit the internet in 2010. His guests included some of the most brilliant minds humanity has ever seen. Through his platform, Joe engaged in conversations with people whose ideas have and will revolutionize our world.

On the other side, Joe gained notoriety for various reasons, and as he grew in success, he stepped on a more than few toes. Joe is the man who is either celebrated or despised, and he wouldn't want it any other way.

Through this complete biography, we left no stone unturned as we tried to solve the equation that is Joe Rogan. However, there is one last variable remaining to be resolved. To do that, we have to let the man speak for himself.

Fortunately, we live in this digital age where his thoughts, beliefs, and ideas are well documented. For your reading pleasure, we are presenting you with Joe Rogan's 'Best of Collection.'

Please, enjoy Joe Rogan's timeless wisdom, unfiltered and raw.

* * *

"No matter how civilized we are and how much society has curbed violent behavior. Human beings still have the same genes they had 10,000 years ago. Our bodies are designed to have a certain amount of physical stress and violence in them. We're designed to run from jaguars and fight to defend our territory."

"I don't care if you're gay, black, Chinese, straight. That means nothing to me. It's all an illusion."

"Never stay in a bad marriage, and don't hang around with psycho coke fiends."

"I have one goal. Surround myself with funny people, and make sure everyone has a good time and works hard."

"I see martial arts as moving forms of meditation. When you're sparring or drilling techniques, you can't think of anything else."

"My act is so completely and totally uncensored that the only way I could really pull it off is if I treat the audience like they're my best friends."

''People want their 15 minutes and are willing to do anything to get it.''

''What's interesting about science is that we're constantly discovering new things about the universe, about ourselves, about our bodies, about diseases, about the possibilities of the future. It's amazing. Science is one of the coolest things about being a human being — without a doubt.''

"The key to happiness doesn't lay in numbers in a bank account but in the way we make others feel and the way they make us feel."

''When you snatch little pieces of other people's lives and try to palm them off as your own, that's more disgusting than anything. Robin Williams is a huge thief. Denis Leary is a huge thief. His whole stand-up career is based on Bill Hicks, a brilliant guy who died years ago.''

''The two things I understand best are stand-up comedy and martial arts. And those things require an ultimate grasp of the truth. You have to be objective about your skills and abilities to compete in both.''

''As a longtime practitioner of yoga and a person who's been involved in physical fitness my whole life, I can tell you, yoga helps you achieve altered states of consciousness. It is not just stretching. The only way you can say that it's stretching is if you haven't done it, or that you haven't done it rigorously for a long period of time.''

''Being a celebrity or anything else where you're really ambitious, it's really a game to see how successful you can get.''

61

"The Universe rewards calculated risk and passion."

"So instead of investing your time in a passion, you've sold your life to work for an uncaring machine that doesn't understand you. That's the problem with our society. And what's the reward? Go home and get a big TV."

"We're constantly re-evaluating the potential for life. We're finding it where we didn't think it could exist, such as volcanic vents and other extreme conditions like under arctic ice. We're finding life in these incredibly harsh and dynamic conditions, so we're having to re-evaluate our own ideas of what's possible on this planet alone."

"When someone comes along and expresses him or herself as freely as they think, people flock to it. They enjoy it."

"People say you can abuse marijuana. You can abuse cheeseburgers. Does that mean we should close Burger Kings."

"You're sort of programmed a certain way because of your environment. That's all you know. But we don't have that anymore because of the internet. Because of the internet we're all communicating with each other all across the board, so you're getting information from people all around the world, hitting a much more diverse slice of culture."

"I think that one of the reasons why people look towards the end of humanity is that people are afraid to die alone. If you die alone, the people you love will miss you, or if they die, you miss them — the sorrow is inevitable. When you truly love someone, the thought of losing them forever is horrible."

''*The people who could most benefit from the self-reflective ego-dissolving qualities of cannabis are the ones that want it to be illegal.*''

"*In all my travels, all my life adventures. I have to say I still don't know what life is, absolutely no clue, and it is a subject that is constantly on my mind. One thing I do know for a fact is that the nicer we are to our fellow human beings, the nicer the universe is to us.*".

"*Reality really is a theater. There's no other way to describe it. It's all so nonsensical, ridiculous, and chaotic.*"

"*If you ever start taking things too seriously, just remember that we are talking monkeys on an organic spaceship flying through the universe.*"

"*To really appreciate life, you got to know you're going to die.*"

"*I realized a long time ago that instead of being jealous you can be inspired and appreciative. It carries more energy to you.*"

"*If you attach your mind to any ideology, you're going to be on a road, and that road may or may not lead you in a good direction. But you're gonna stay on that road because you are attached to an ideology. It could be a terrible road, but you stick with it regardless of rational thinking.*"

"*Live your life like you're the hero in your own movie. Pretend that your life was a movie and it started now, what would the hero do? What would the person that you respect do? What would the person* that you admire, and inspire you to do? Do that."

"Build confidence and momentum with each good decision you make from here on out and choose to be inspired."

"Greatness and madness are next-door neighbors and they often borrow each other's sugar."

"We have to start treating each other as if we are treating ourselves living another life."

"We define ourselves far too often by our past failures. That's not you. You are this person right now. You're the person who has learned from those failures."

"If you can control what you eat, you can control all other aspects of your life."

"It's very important to help people figure out how to manage life, to help people figure out how to think, help inspire them, help show them what can be gained from setting goals and achieving them and that excellent feeling and that becomes contagious."

"Excellence in anything increases your potential in everything."

"By putting yourself in that intense form of stress, it makes regular life more peaceful."

"So many people are selling their life to sit in a box and work for a machine. An uncaring machine that demands productivity that doesn't understand you and doesn't want to understand you. There's *no natural behavior."*

"All the time that you spend complaining, you could instead be hustling. You could be chasing your dream. You could be figuring out what you're doing wrong and improving your life."

"Your attitude has a giant effect not just on your life, but on other people's lives around you."

"If things aren't going the way you want them to go, then do something about it. Quit talking about your problems and go out and do something to fix them."

"Kindness is one of the best gifts you can bestow. We know that inherently that feels great."

"I want to make sure that everything that I'm creating, I'm creating it so other people get enjoyment out of it. And that's the reward that you get for that."

"Haters are all failures. It's 100% across the board. No one who is truly brilliant at anything is a hater."

"You can't measure what's inside a man's heart."

"The quicker we all realize that we've been taught how to live life by the people that were operating on the momentum of an ignorant past the quicker we can move to a global ethic of community that doesn't value invented borders or the monopolization of natural resources, but rather the goal of a happier more loving humanity."

65

"I've been inspired by a shitload of people in my life so if there's ever anybody that I can inspire, to me that's a huge gift. To be able to turn that back around."

"Here's the craziest thing about life, this is the thing that nobody really considers. You know as much about what life is all about as anybody who's ever lived, ever."

"One of the things that happened is I did a lot of shitty gigs. When you do a bunch of shitty bar gigs you have to get used to people yelling at you, you're used to thinking on the fly, to dealing with weird situations."

"Get better at whatever you're doing. So what if you suck at it now. Everybody sucks at everything when they start. But if you love it, and don't lie to yourself, then get better at it."

"Do things that are difficult. It's very important to struggle. You don't get to know yourself without struggle. You don't know who you are until you get tested."

"Martial arts are a vehicle for developing your human potential."

"You are one minuscule piece of a never-ending cycle. In fact, you're not even a piece. You're just a holder for billions and billions of other pieces. Whether that's organic components, living organisms inside your body, bacteria, or whatever it is, you're just part of the soup of the universe, so just try to enjoy what's good about it."

"There are only two reasons that you hate gay marriage. One, you're dumb, or two, you're secretly worried that dicks are delicious."

''The people I know that have the hardest time keeping it together emotionally are people that don't workout.''

''There's a very famous Miyamoto Musashi quote.
  "Once you understand the way broadly, you can see it in all things."
The idea is once you understand what excellence is all about, whether it's in painting, or carpentry or martial arts, that you see how that excellence manifests itself in any discipline. I think that all the different things that I do enhance all the other things that I do.''

''The number one reason why marijuana is illegal is because the Pharma Cartel does not want you to grow your own medicine. The Declaration of Independence was written on hemp paper. The first car ever made ran on hemp oil. Hemp seeds are also the healthiest food on the planet with the highest protein content out of any plant.''

''Our entire civilization is built on a foundation of unfixable bullshit.''

''If you attach your mind to any ideology, you're going to be on a road, and that road may or may not lead you in a good direction. But you're gonna stay on that road because you are attached to an ideology. It could be a terrible road, but you stick with it regardless of rational thinking.''

''I'll go to church with anyone who's willing to smoke pot and look through a telescope with me.''

''We live in a society that makes it really easy for these pussies to get by.''

''This country has a mental health problem disguised as a gun *problem, and a tyranny problem disguised as a security problem.''*

''It's a weird experience when you're just trying to talk openly about how you think psychedelic drugs and marijuana are beneficial, or a lot of different drugs, especially plant-based ones, can be beneficial. Especially those ones that have some connection to organic life, I feel like you can learn something from them, from mushrooms, from peyote, from marijuana. They can be used as a tool.''

''The beautiful thing about podcasting is it's just talking. It can be funny, or it can be terrifying. It can be sweet. It can be obnoxious. It almost has no definitive form. In that sense it's one of the best ways to explore an idea, and certainly much less limiting than trying to express the same idea in stand up comedy. For some ideas stand up is best, but it's really, really nice to have podcasts as well.''

''I always try to look at conflicts from as many different angles as is humanly possible, and in a lot of ways there is no one answer.''

''Like bees creating a beehive or ants creating an anthill we're all moving along creating something and we're not sure what it is.''

''I don't know much about the music business, but for just general advice for someone trying to create things, as simple as this sounds, I think the best thing you can do is constantly try to improve upon your work. Always focus on that first and foremost, and leave everything else (marketing, image) completely secondary. Obviously, easier said than done when you're trying to make a living, but if you can move along those lines and earnestly try to make things that you really enjoy it can only benefit you in the long run.''

''There's a lot of people that I disagree with that I think I could have interesting conversations with. What I don't want to get into is manufactured conflict. I would much rather talk to someone like Dr. Rhonda Patrick or Randall Carlson and be mesmerized by the information.

I guess in a way that's selfish, or maybe not objective of me. The older (and hopefully wiser) I get the less interested I am in conflict. I don't mind disagreeing with people in a civil way, but I definitely don't want to go out of my way to have an argument unless it's a really important subject.''

''I brought something back from those experiences [with drugs] which made me softer, open to other ideas. And I've learned from listening to other people talk about their experiences, from listening to Bill Hicks or reading Terrence McKenna or Aldous Huxley and Timothy Leary. But there's always some dumb cop out there who says "We don't need another legal drug and there's psychological addiction and blah blah blah.''

''I don't really like actors. Actors are like terrible comedians with no punch lines. It's all about them. They talk about themselves all the time. They bore the sh — t out of you.''

''People do always try to smoke pot with me. But I think some of those people are cops.''

''I thought eventually I'd have a family and I really didn't want to be a loser like that guy in his 40s still shopping his band's shitty demo tapes around.''

''People for the most part can smell lies, at least I thought that until

69

I saw audiences applaud at Carlos Mencia.''

''Now obviously popularity isn't everything when it comes to stand up comedy, but the art form itself is better today than it ever has before. I think there are more great comics. I think the standard is higher.

The critical analysis is a little harsher, but that is also good. Maybe people have a higher standard than before, maybe they are a little more judgmental, a little more brutal, that makes people work harder. It makes the stand up better.''

''I really feel like it's a travesty to make a child famous. I really do.''

"Reality really is a theatre. There's no other way to describe it. It's all so nonsensical, ridiculous and chaotic."

"I love a success story, but even more than a success story; I like a dude who fuc*s his life up and gets his life together again story."

"It's very important to help people figure out how to manage life, to help people figure out how to think, help inspire them, help show them what can be gained from setting goals and achieving them and that excellent feeling — and that becomes contagious."

"Work for that feeling that you have accomplished something...Don't waste your time on this earth without making a mark."

"There's only one way to get good at anything: You surround yourself with the bad motherfuc**rs who are doing exactly what you do and you force yourself to keep up and inspire each other."

About the Author

James J. Marsden is an American researcher, librarian, and author. He was born in San Diego at the height of the hippie movement.

Born and raised with love and compassion, his loving parents instilled those two values in him from the moment his mother brought him into this world. From the earliest age, he loved surfing, the beach, and the ocean. Little Jamie would often sit on the La Jolla Shores, daydreaming about becoming a professional surfer.

Although surfing remained his first love, in his early teenage years, James developed a keen interest in music and painting. Not surprisingly, his mother was a dancer and a painter, and his father was a musician and a writer.

Coming from an artistic family, James's path seemed predestined. He formed his first band while still in elementary school. The boys who formed the original lineup were friends first and foremost.

From the moment they played their first gig in the backyard, they swore an oath. The boys agreed to stop performing together before allowing anything to come between them and their friendship.

Throughout the entire high school, they stayed together and got better and better, often dreaming of playing in front of hundreds of thousands of screaming fans.

Unfortunately, it wasn't meant to be. Jamie's best friend and the band's lead singer passed away in a tragic accident, and things were never the same again. Jamie spent the next year dealing with a tragic loss, and although he would never really recover, he learned how to move on despite the pain.

During that time, he spent most of the time in his home, reading books as that was the only form of escapism that could provide comfort. It was in these darkest moments that Jamie discovered his profound love for literature, and reading quickly became his favorite activity.

Encouraged by his parents to explore and venture into the world, he decided to move to Europe just one day after turning 21.

With nothing more than dreams and aspirations in his back pocket, James moved to Spain and later to Portugal, where he would teach surfing classes to those eager to explore the waves and the ocean. In addition, James was a guitar teacher for a short while, supporting himself in any way he could.

In fact, because of the dire financial situation at the time, James worked various jobs with more or less success. Although he never saw himself working a nine-to-five corporate job, the necessity prevailed over principles. James started his corporate career as an intern in a telemarketing company before transferring to the sales department.

In a moment of true serendipity, James met a man who changed his life. The man worked as a broker, and he introduced James to a completely new world — The world of financial markets.

For the next two decades, James worked his way up the corporate ladder.

After a global financial crisis and the market crash in 2008, disillusioned with the current state of affairs, James decided to retire and leave the corporate world behind him.

Since then, James has devoted most of his time engaging in activities that 'fuel his soul' and bring him unmitigated joy. He spends most of his time researching, reading, writing, and collecting books for his private library. Even though he doesn't believe in the work-life balance, when he is not working, James enjoys listening to his vinyl records with a glass of bourbon whiskey and his favorite Churchill cigar in hand.

Made in the USA
Monee, IL
23 November 2023

20ec501f-ce29-4b02-934c-53c1d2dfdc38R01